EXPLORER BOOKS

TREASURE

by
Jean Waricha

D0043715

Published by The Trumpet Club
666 Fifth Avenue, New York, New York 10103

ISBN: 0-440-84592-0

Printed in the United States of America
October 1991

10 9 8 7 6 5 4 3 2 1
CW

PHOTOGRAPH CREDITS

p. 23: top, The Bettmann Archive; *bottom,* The Bettmann Archive.   *p. 24:* The
Bettmann Archive.   *p. 25:* The Bettmann Archive; *inset,* The Bettmann Archive.
p. 26: top, UPI/Bettmann; *bottom,* UPI/Bettmann.   *p. 27:* UPI/Bettmann.   *p. 28:
top,* © 1986 Woods Hole Oceanographic Institution; *bottom,* UPI/Bettmann News-
photos.   *p. 29: top,* © 1985 Carl Roessler/FPG International; *bottom,* Copyright ©
Al Grotell 1990.   *p. 30: top,* Jill M. Wallin ©/FPG International; *bottom,* J & C
Church/FPG International.

Cover: The Image Bank

Contents

To my sister—for all her encouragement

Introduction

What do you think of when you hear the word treasure? Many people think of pirate gold, sunken Spanish ships, or jewels hidden on some forgotten island. Others think of lost cities and the stolen riches of faraway exotic places and mythical lands. But treasure doesn't always mean gold and jewels. Treasure can be a book, a letter, a stamp, a piece of pottery, a kind of spice, even an old comic book. Treasure is simply anything that someone values enough to spend money, time, effort, and sometimes lives to acquire.

People have searched for treasure throughout history. The desire for treasure led explorers like Marco Polo, Columbus, Cortés, and others to sail their ships into the unknown and discover new worlds.

In this book, you will read about many different kinds of treasure and about people who have spent their lives searching for it. You'll meet Mel Fisher of Key West, Florida, who gambled everything on his hunch that he could find a fabulous sunken treasure that would make him a millionaire. And you'll learn about Dr. Robert Ballard, who devoted himself to the search for the famous ship the *Titanic*— even though he didn't want to take a single object away from the ship. And you will see that the hunt for treasure is the search for wealth, but it is also the search for adventure!

1

Pirates Ahoy!

"Where gold goes, blood flows." This is an old folk saying, and it describes the lives of some treasure-hunting pirates perfectly!

Following Columbus's voyages to the New World, during the 1500's Spain set up colonies in North and South America. Soon the colonists began to gather all the gold, silver, and gems they could find to send back to Spain. Each year three fleets of treasure-filled ships were sent across the ocean, escorted by warships. These fleets were naturally at the mercy of pirates.

Pirates were sailors who attacked and robbed ships on the high seas. When most people think of pirates, they think of evil-hearted men who sailed under the skull-and-crossbones flag and made people walk the plank. They believe all pirates wore bright red bandannas, gold earrings, black eye patches, and often had wooden legs. These beliefs are very common, but most of them aren't really true.

Some pirates *were* evil monsters, but most of them were not. The stories we associate with pirates—tales of terror, walking the plank, and leaving prisoners marooned on desert islands— are mostly exaggerations. Many pirates started out as ordinary sailors. But they didn't get paid much for their hard work. Sometimes they were led into dangerous situations by ship captains who cared nothing about their safety. To some sailors, becoming a pirate was the only way to escape the sailor's hard life.

Another mistaken notion people have is that pirates often built huge fortunes. The truth is, very few pirates became truly rich. Most of them gambled or drank away their money.

Tales of buried treasure are also exaggerated. A typical treasure chest weighed about 50 pounds— *empty.* If it were filled with gold coins, it would weigh some 2,500 pounds. It would take a group of strong men to lift such a chest, so it would be impossible for one man to bury it secretly by himself.

Pirates were also seen as outlaws, ruthless men who thought they were above the law. In fact, every pirate ship had a set of laws called the Ship's Articles. Each pirate had to put his signature at the bottom of this document. A circle was drawn, then each pirate signed his name or made his mark near the circle.

These laws guaranteed the rights of pirates and determined how the stolen treasure would be divided. After signing, the men chose a flag. Sometimes they chose the skull and crossbones, also known as the Jolly Roger, but more often they chose a plain black flag. Sometimes they chose a red flag with a beer mug on it!

There were, of course, some truly dangerous pirates. The most notorious, ruthless, and brutal pirate who ever lived was Edward Teach, better known as Blackbeard. It was Blackbeard's career that gave rise to the wildest pirate legends we hear today.

Teach grew up in the streets of Bristol, England. His parents died when he was very young. He escaped from his poor life in England by becoming a cabin boy on a ship that was sailing to the West Indies. Once there, he deserted the ship and became an apprentice pirate. He made a reputation for himself as a cruel and dirty fighter. Before long he set out on his own, calling himself Blackbeard. He wanted a name that would terrify people.

Blackbeard carefully made himself into the picture of his name. He grew a beard that covered his entire face and hung down to his belt buckle. People couldn't tell where his beard ended and his hair began. His beard and hair were usually matted with grease because he wiped his hands on them after eating. As if this weren't bad enough, his clothes, hands, and face were caked with garbage, slime, and blood. Blackbeard wanted his appearance to strike fear and terror into the hearts of all those who saw him—and it did!

Sometimes when Blackbeard boarded a ship, he made himself even more terrifying by putting lighted matches in his beard. The matches would sizzle, crackle, and fill the air with sulfur fumes. The crew of the ship he had attacked would see this frightening madman and quickly surrender. Blackbeard would keep the ship, divide the loot among his men, then set the crew ashore.

Blackbeard soon had a huge pirate fleet and the best crew of pirates around. He sailed the Atlantic coast from Maine and Nova Scotia to the Caribbean Islands. It is believed that he buried most of his share of the treasure that he stole from the British and the Spanish somewhere in that area.

The more successful Blackbeard was, the more determined the British and Spanish were to capture him. Finally, in 1718 the British sent a special fleet of ships after him. Blackbeard avoided the fleet and hid out in an inlet off the coast of North and South Carolina. On the afternoon of November 21, 1718, Blackbeard and his crew were attacked by two English warships. Blackbeard outsailed, outmaneuvered, and outfought the British, but he still lost the battle.

In the fight, each member of Blackbeard's crew used a kind of sword called a *cutlass*. This was the pirate's preferred weapon. The cutlass weighed about 10 pounds, which is the same weight as five baseball bats. Swinging this heavy weapon back and forth often made the pirates very tired. The English sailors, on the other hand, used *rapiers*, which are thin-bladed, lightweight swords.

After a half hour of fighting, Blackbeard's pirates were quite tired. The English realized their advantage and closed in for the kill. Soon Blackbeard was the only pirate left standing. But in the end he, too, was killed.

Blackbeard's ships were searched, but no treasure was found. What happened to all the riches he had stolen? Some people believe Blackbeard knew that he was going to be captured, so he hid his fortune somewhere on the coast of North or South Carolina. But he didn't leave a map or any other clue. Today treasure hunters are still searching for Blackbeard's hidden treasure.

Although Blackbeard's treasure is still lost, his skull survives. After killing Blackbeard, the English cut off his head and hung it from the ship's mast. A wealthy merchant bought the skull and had both the inside and the outside coated with silver. Drinking a pint of wine from Blackbeard's skull soon became a great thrill. Today the skull is owned by an American treasure hunter.

Another famous pirate was William Kidd, better known as Captain Kidd. Kidd is supposed to have buried more treasure than any other pirate. The adventures of Captain Kidd began in 1695 when he was hired by the English as a *privateer*. A privateer was a pirate who was hired by one country to raid another country's ships. But his work as a privateer was a disaster. His crew became more and more rebellious with every batch of gold they seized. They didn't want to turn the riches over to the English. They wanted to keep it for themselves. Finally Kidd began to attack any and all treasure ships. This made him an enemy of the British.

Kidd was declared an outlaw and eventually captured. He was then put on trial and sentenced to death. On the day of his execution, Kidd got drunk and staggered toward the gallows. Crowds of spectators lined the streets, screaming for gold. (Sometimes pirates who were about to be hanged threw treasures to the crowd.) When the procession reached the gallows, the hangman put the rope around Kidd's neck and pushed him off the platform. Kidd dangled from the rope awhile, and then it snapped. Kidd fell into the mud, causing a loud shriek to go up from the crowd. He was taken to the gallows a second time and finally hanged.

After Kidd's death his body was cut down and chained to a post, where the waves washed over it for three days and three nights. The body was then taken down, painted with tar, and placed in an iron framework so that the bones would stay in place when the body rotted. Finally, Kidd's body was displayed on a high post, where ships sailing in and out of London could see it. It was meant to be a warning: No treasure-stealing pirates allowed! No one knows how long the rotting corpse swung there. Some say it remained there for years!

Although some of Kidd's treasure was found and seized by the British government, his real treasure trove was never located. When he died, Kidd took the secret of the treasure's location with him.

During the 1920's and 1930's, four different maps showing the location of Kidd's treasure island were found. Each was signed in a handwriting that people said looked like Kidd's. One of these maps, the most detailed, showed that his treasure island was somewhere in the China Sea.

Another map showed an island that looks very much like Oak Island, which is located on Mahone Bay in Nova Scotia, Canada. Oak Island is 2½ miles long and 1 mile wide. It is an out-of-the-way island with few people, which makes it a perfect place to bury treasure. Oak Island is also the location of a mysterious pit that is sometimes called the money pit.

In 1785, three boys were hunting on Oak Island when they noticed that one branch of an old tree seemed more worn than the others. This branch looked as if it had been used to lift something heavy. Beneath the worn branch the ground was caved-in and soft, as if something had been buried there.

The next day the boys returned with shovels and began to dig. At a depth of 10 feet, they hit something hard. It was a set of wooden planks. But when they pulled the planks away, there was nothing there—just more dirt. They continued to dig and found a similar set of wooden planks at 20 feet, at 30 feet, and again at 40 feet. They had to stop at this point. Without professional help or special equipment, they could go no deeper.

The boys were forced to give up their dig, but they were convinced that they had found a hiding place for treasure. The story of the money pit spread. Many people believed it was the hiding place of Captain Kidd's fortune. Years later, another treasure hunter heard this story and continued the dig. When he had dug 90 feet deep, he found that there was a huge stone blocking the path. When he removed it, the tunnel filled with water! Although the treasure hunter spent weeks trying to bail out the water, the task became impossible and he gave up. No more digging was done in the pit for many years.

In 1893, the Oak Island Treasure Company was formed by another treasure hunter. He reopened the Oak Island pit, but it again filled with water. The Treasure Company wanted to stop the flow of seawater into the pit. They used dynamite to blow holes around the pit and drain the water. One hundred and sixty pounds of dynamite were used to blast three separate holes, but the money pit remained flooded. Unfortunately, the Treasure Company soon ran out of money and gave up.

Since then, no one has been able to reach the bottom of the pit. One company was able to send underwater cameras into the flooded area. The cameras went into a cave that was about 200 feet below the surface. There they took pictures of what seemed to be three metal chests with a cut-off hand lying nearby.

Today the mystery of what is buried in the Oak Island money pit remains unsolved. Many people who dig there believe it is filled with millions of dollars in stolen riches. But it's possible that the money pit is just another pirate legend.

2

Deep-Sea Searching

No one knows when the search for sunken treasure first began. In the ancient Middle East, divers gathered shellfish from the ocean floor to make purple dye. The dye was very expensive because it took *6,000* shellfish to make *one* drop. The color purple was worn only by Roman emperors, and in those days Rome controlled all of the land around the Mediterranean Sea.

The early Egyptians searched the sea for mother-of-pearl, which they used to make masks for mummies. Greek divers searched the Mediterranean Sea for sponges. Sponges were valuable because they were used in medicine, as canteens for soldiers, and as padding for armor.

In China, the red coral brought up by divers was used as jewelry by wealthy Chinese. Japanese divers withstood extremely cold water to bring up pearls. These divers could stay underwater for a very long time on only one lungful of air. Sometimes they wore goggles made of tortoise shells that had been rubbed thin enough to allow them to see through the water.

Divers in ancient Rome dived to *salvage,* or save, the riches carried by sunken ships. The early Roman ships were poorly made, and they frequently ended up on the ocean floor. But these divers could remain underwater for only two or three minutes at a time. This made it impossible for them to rescue most of the contents of the ships.

People began to experiment with ways of staying underwater for longer periods. During the 1500's, Leonardo da Vinci drew a sketch of a swimmer wearing a diving mask, a snorkel-like device, and flippers. Leonardo never tried out his idea, however.

The first practical invention to aid underwater exploration was the *diving bell.* It was invented in 1538 but did not come into common use until the 1600's. A diving bell was like a large tub or bucket that was forced into the water with the open end down. Air would be trapped inside it. A diver would swim to the bucket when his air supply ran out, stick his head inside, and get a breath. But the diving bell contained only a limited amount of air. If a diver used it too often, he would pass out from lack of oxygen. Sometimes the bell was even swept away in the current!

In 1839, the world's first diving suit was invented by Augustus Siebe. It was little more than a metal helmet with windows, which was then attached to a metal jacket. Air was pumped into the helmet through hoses connected to it from a ship. This helmet allowed divers to breathe underwater and stay down longer. But there were problems with this invention, too. The helmet was so heavy and clumsy for the diver to swim in that he could only walk along the ocean floor. Also, the diver couldn't walk farther than the length of the air hose that connected the helmet to the ship. If the hose got snagged or twisted, the diver lost his air supply.

In 1865, two Frenchmen invented the first *SCUBA* (Self-Contained Underwater Breathing Apparatus). The earliest device was simply a tank on the diver's back that had been filled with compressed air. A tube went from the tank to the diver's mouth. Although this was a step in the right direction, the early SCUBAs didn't work well. The tank held very little air. Also, the inventors didn't realize that their invention could make underwater movement easier. As a result, divers continued to wear heavy shoes and weights that held them on the ocean bottom.

In 1943, Jacques-Yves Cousteau, the well-known deep-sea explorer, and Emil Gagnan, an engineer, perfected the SCUBA. They called their device the *Aqua-lung*. The Aqua-lung held more air, and it allowed divers to breathe comfortably underwater for longer periods. Rubber fins had been perfected in 1933. Diving goggles had been improved, too. Instead of two pieces of distorting, uncomfortable glass on a rubber strap, a single-glass unit that also covered the nose was invented. When the Aqua-lung was combined with a diving mask and rubber fins, divers found that they could now move underwater with ease and speed.

Although this equipment made the search for underwater treasure possible, it was (and is) still dangerous and very difficult work. After all, most wrecked ships lie on the ocean bottom in total darkness—some as many as 2 miles underwater.

Rough weather, ocean swells, and dangerous currents can make the search for ships almost impossible. Even when a ship lies in shallow water, sudden changes in the weather can make exploration very dangerous. Divers sometimes meet killer sharks, whales, or stingrays. Coral reefs have jagged edges that can be dangerous. Also, there is always the danger of a diver's SCUBA gear failing.

Today divers have many new tools to help them in their search for underwater treasure. For example, they often use remote-control cameras to locate treasure in the ocean. A special underwater camera is built onto a sturdy platform. The platform can be sent very deep, where divers can't easily go. The *magnetometer* is also a useful tool. It can detect any iron object under the water. Since ships usually have iron in them, the magnetometer can lead treasure hunters directly to sunken ships. In addition, modern treasure hunters use computers, underwater robots that can go deeper than humans can, and tracking devices that search the ocean floor. Computerized library records and microfilm systems have made it easier to research old records and maps.

This new equipment has greatly improved treasure hunting, but it has also made it more and more expensive. It can cost thousands of dollars a day to hire divers, rent ships, and provide all the special equipment treasure hunters and divers need. Sometimes the value of the treasure isn't worth the time and effort spent in recovering it. For many divers, however, the *excitement* is the big payoff!

3

Mel Fisher's Search for
the *Atocha*

Two divers stood on the deck of a salvage boat anchored in the Gulf of Mexico off the Florida Keys. They adjusted their diving masks and checked their cylinder-shaped oxygen tanks. This could be the day! They glanced at each other nervously. A metal detector on board had identified something in the water below, and they were going to investigate it.

Both divers jumped into the warm sea feetfirst and quickly descended to a depth of about 55 feet. Visibility was good. When they reached bottom, one diver fanned the sand with his hand. Coins appeared! The other diver used a hand-held metal detector to examine a large mound of coral. The detector suddenly went crazy. When the two divers took a closer look at the ocean bottom, they saw planks of wood. These looked like the hull of a ship. On top of the planks, covered with coral, were hundreds of bars of silver.

This discovery marked the end of Mel Fisher's long search for the wreck of the lost Spanish galleon, the *Atocha*. Fisher had been looking for the wreck for 16 years! Originally christened *Nuestra Señora de Atocha*, or *Our Lady of Atocha*, the ship sank in a hurricane in 1622. Fisher had overcome personal tragedy, frustration, and sacrifice to realize his dream of finding the *Atocha*'s sunken riches. In the end, his search would lead to a treasure of nearly $200 million in gold, silver, and emeralds!

The story of the *Atocha* started in the 1600's. On September 4, 1622, a Spanish merchant fleet left Havana, Cuba, for Spain during the hurricane season. The fleet was loaded with gold, silver, and tobacco that had been found in the New World. Armed Spanish galleons protected the rich cargo from pirates and other enemies.

The *Atocha* was built to be a guard ship for the Spanish fleet leaving for Spain in 1622. Guard ships were like any other ships in the fleet, except that they were heavily armed and ready for battle. The *Atocha*, along with three other guard ships, was built in the New World. It was the last of the four ships to be constructed. Because the builder was behind schedule, he became careless. He substituted mahogany for oak in some of the ship's beams. Mahogany breaks under stress, while oak bends. The builder also skimped on nails and spikes. He used only two where five were needed, for example. The ship and its passengers were doomed from the start.

The *Atocha* took up its position at the end of the fleet. The ship carried 20 bronze cannons, 60 muskets, and a full supply of powder and shot. With all that protection, the guard ship was thought to be very safe. The ship's registered cargo included 900 silver bars, 161 gold disks and bars, and about 255,000 silver coins. Among the passengers were wealthy Spanish merchants who were taking their wives and teenage daughters home to Spain.

On the day the fleet left home port, the weather was serene and quiet, with a wind that was just right for sailing. But the next day things turned ugly. The waves became so high that the ships had difficulty staying on course. By noon the ships were being pounded by the fierce winds, and the towering waves threatened to swallow them. The terrified passengers prayed for safety.

Suddenly the wind took an abrupt shift. Masts split and fell into the sea. Sails ripped apart like wet tissue paper, and rudders broke, leaving the ships to drift at the mercy of the storm. Although some of the ships managed to work clear of land, eight had been damaged so badly that they were wrecked. The *Atocha* was among these.

Stripped of many of its sails, the *Atocha* hit the reefs along the coast of the Florida Keys. Its hull split apart, and the ship sank into the deep water suddenly and without a trace. Of the 265 passengers who were on board, only 5 survived.

Within weeks after the *Atocha* sank, the Spanish attempted to salvage the wreck, but divers could stay down only as long as the air in their lungs held out. They were unable to open the hatches of the ship or work their way into the hold. Soon a second hurricane swept through the Keys and tore the sunken *Atocha* apart. The upper portion of the ship was carried north, and much of its gold, silver, and jewelry was scattered along the way. The treasure of the *Atocha* remained at the bottom of the sea for centuries. Nobody could find it, although many tried.

Mel Fisher, the man who finally found the *Atocha,* was born in a small Midwestern town far from the ocean. He had read Robert Louis Stevenson's *Treasure Island* and dreamed of finding pirate treasure and sunken ships. He first began to look for treasure when he was 11 years old. In his handmade diving helmet, which consisted of an old paint can with a hole cut in the side and covered with glass, Mel would carefully duck under the water and look around. He could do this only for a minute at a time. But his enthusiasm for both diving and treasure hunting grew as he became older. When he finished high school, he moved to California and opened a store that sold diving equipment.

During the 1960's, Mel Fisher read about the *Atocha* disaster and became determined to find the lost treasure ship. Fisher sold his home and boat in California and headed for the Florida Keys with his wife and children. After getting settled, he bought a new boat and began to search.

Fisher soon faced a major problem, however. Sunken treasure was usually buried deep in the sand, and removing the sand was difficult. Most divers used an air hose to blow the sand away, but this made the water so murky that they could barely see a few inches in front of them.

Fisher solved this problem by inventing a device known as the *mailbox*, which removed the sand and left the water clear. He made it by fitting a large metal box over a ship's propellers. When the propellers were turned on, clear surface water was forced to the bottom of the sea. This made it easier to see the sandy bottom. The force of the water cleared the sand away, and exposed any objects that were hidden underneath.

Mel Fisher searched the Florida Keys for years without finding a trace of the vanished *Atocha*. Sometimes he and his team uncovered parts of sunken ships, a few gold coins, or even a cannon. But none of these belonged to the *Atocha*. Fisher soon discovered why he was having so little luck.

Early in 1970, Eugene Lyon, one of Fisher's friends, discovered that he had been looking in the wrong place. Lyon had been translating some Spanish documents concerning shipwrecks in the Florida Keys, as well as studying old maps of Florida. These documents were very hard to read. The handwriting wasn't like modern script; it was all circles and curlicues. The ink had faded completely in spots, and many of the sentences had no punctuation. All the same, Lyon continued to work on the documents until he was sure he knew where the *Atocha* could be found. He then wrote to Fisher and told him that the *Atocha,* as well as another ship, the *Santa Margarita,* had sunk near the Marquesas Keys. This is a group of islands located miles from where Fisher had been searching.

With this information, Fisher moved his team to the new site and began the search all over again. They began to make discoveries almost immediately. His divers found a long gold chain, silver coins, and an anchor. Fisher knew in his heart that these were all from the *Atocha.* But so far there was no real proof of this. Furthermore, Fisher was troubled by what he *couldn't* find. Where was the huge stone that was used as ballast? *Ballast* stones were huge boulders placed in the bottom of the ship to help keep it upright in the water.

Fisher continued to find small objects all through 1972, but nothing of any real importance turned up. Then, in 1973, his divers began to bring up silver bars. These bars were stamped with an identification number. These numbers matched perfectly a list of items that were known to be on the *Atocha.* Mel Fisher had finally found the proof he needed! He was closer than ever to finding the *Atocha.* Before his search ended, though, he would also find trouble and tragedy.

In August 1973, Fisher allowed visitors to tour the site of his underwater search. During one of these visits, an 11-year-old boy somehow fell into the water. He was sucked into the boat's propellers before anyone could reach him. The boy died on his way to the hospital. Shaken and discouraged, Fisher tightened security and vowed that this would never happen again. Two years later, however, he suffered another tragedy. This time it was closer to home.

The search team had just brought up a cannon, and everyone was sure they were close to discovering the wrecked *Atocha* itself. One of Fisher's search boats, the *Northwind,* dropped anchor at the site for the night. During the night the boat sprang a leak, and water poured into it. No one realized what was happening. Without warning, it tipped on its side and began to sink. Eleven people were on board. Eight of them managed to escape, but three crew members were trapped inside the boat. Mel Fisher's son Dirk and Dirk's wife, Angel, drowned that night.

Mel Fisher's quest for treasure had now cost the lives of a young boy, his own son, and his daughter-in-law. He and his wife, Dolores, were devastated. Perhaps it was time to give up their search. Months went by before Fisher and his wife could go on. But they did go on. Finally, in 1985, Mel Fisher's search ended. The *Atocha,* with its treasure, was found resting on the ocean floor in 55 feet of water. It was in an area Fisher had searched years earlier. Fisher also discovered the *Santa Margarita* in nearby waters. All together, he uncovered an enormous treasure—valued at more than $200 million.

Salvage work began immediately. Television and newspaper reporters crowded on the boats, often shouting out questions. Divers began bringing up silver bars that were loaded into giant baskets made out of supermarket shopping carts from which the wheels had been removed. Fisher loaded so many silver bars onto one boat that he thought it would sink.

Soon underwater archaeologists began to show up at the site to study and record the wreck. Meanwhile, Fisher's divers brought up 166 gold bars, 950 silver bars, and more than 15 solid gold chains. The divers also found emeralds. One of these emeralds was as big as a Tootsie Roll!

One of the most interesting gold objects the divers found was a "poison cup." The inside of the cup contained a small wire basket that held a *bezoar,* a small stonelike lump that is sometimes formed in the intestines of a goat or llama. People believed that a bezoar was capable of soaking up arsenic, a kind of poison. If someone poured an arsenic-poisoned drink into the cup, the bezoar was supposed to absorb it and the drinker would remain unharmed.

Much of the riches Fisher found in the *Atocha* was sold or divided among the people who had invested in his underwater adventures. Everyone ended up making money. But even though Mel Fisher became a millionaire several times over, he didn't stop hunting for treasure. He soon began to research the location of another treasure ship, the *Adventure!*

The famous pirate Blackbeard set his beard and hair on fire to scare his enemies.

Although people believe the pirate Captain Kidd buried many treasure chests, there is no proof.

A diving bell.

Divers using early diving suits.

The first diving suits were heavy and uncomfortable. A long air hose was attached to the helmet to allow the diver to breathe.

More than 100 tons of gold were hidden by the German government in an old salt mine in Merkers, Germany, during World War II.

Priceless paintings were also found in Merkers Mine.

A diver lifts a basket filled with silver bars found in the sunken wreck of the *Atocha*.

The small robot called Jason Junior (JJ) explores and
photographs the *Titanic.*

This photograph of a chandelier in the *Titanic* was taken by
JJ's camera.

Divers explore a wrecked ship in the waters off the Philippines.

This diver peeks through what used to be a porthole.

These coral-encrusted forms look like modern sculptures, but the one at the top is the gun of a battleship. At the bottom is a ship's propeller.

4

The *Titanic*—Search and Discovery

Perhaps the greatest and most thrilling story of underwater search was the discovery of the SS *Titanic*. The *Titanic* was one of three huge ocean liners that had been built to provide passengers with every comfort and luxury they could desire while at sea. Tragically, on its first voyage from England to New York in 1912, it collided with an iceberg and sank. Many years afterward, treasure hunters were still wondering where the wreck was. Could it be raised? What treasures would be found in it? Some people thought that the bodies of those who died when the ship sank were still on the ocean bottom, preserved by the cold water.

The *Titanic* was the largest ship built at that time. When it was launched, 22 tons of soap, grease, and train oil were used to slide it into the water. A team of twenty horses was needed just to pull one of the ship's anchors. Three million rivets were hammered into its hull. The ship could carry enough food to feed a small town for several months. It was almost as long as four city blocks and as tall as an eleven-story building. It was thought to be unsinkable.

On Wednesday, April 10, 1912, the *Titanic* left Southampton, England, on its first, or maiden, voyage to New York. The ship's passenger list included some of the wealthiest people in the world. Mr. and Mrs. Jacob Astor, said to be the world's richest couple, paid $5,000 for their first-class rooms. Other important people on board included Isidor Straus, one of the brothers who owned Macy's department store, and his wife. Another famous passenger was Washington Augustus Roebling, the man most responsible for building the Brooklyn Bridge.

The millionaires who were on board the *Titanic* brought along their wives, children, servants, and mountains of luggage. A brand-new Renault automobile was in the hold of the ship. One passenger is said to have had an $11,000 diamond necklace and 55 pounds of gold bullion locked in one of the ship's four safes. One of the most valuable objects on board was a book entitled *The Rubáiyát of Omar Khayyám*. The cover of this book was studded with thousands of diamonds, rubies, and pearls. Some experts have estimated that more than $300 million worth of jewelry and other objects were aboard the ship when it sank.

The *Titanic* was magnificent, and its maiden voyage was accompanied by great excitement. But some people believed it was jinxed. Rumors claimed that there was a cursed mummy in the hold, or that there was an evil Buddha aboard. There were whispers that the ship was unlucky. On the day the *Titanic* left the dock, the suction from its three propellers pulled a smaller boat from its mooring. Disaster was avoided only by stopping the *Titanic*'s engines.

By the morning of April 12, the *Titanic* was well out into the Atlantic, sailing at a speed of 21 knots. (Measuring a boat's speed in *knots* is like checking a car's speed in *miles per hour*. Although 21 knots may not seem fast, even today the speediest ocean liners do not travel much faster.) On Sunday, April 14, the captain of the *Titanic* received a radio message warning him that there was ice ahead. Several more warnings of ice came throughout the day. The temperature began to drop. Captain Edward J. Smith appeared unconcerned and gave no orders to slow the speed of the ship. His only precaution was to order the lookout man at the very top of the ship, in what was called the *crow's nest*, to keep a careful watch for icebergs.

At about 11:40 P.M., the lookout man saw an iceberg directly in front of the *Titanic*. He immediately rang the warning bell and telephoned the bridge. The first officer took steps to avoid an accident, but the iceberg and the *Titanic* collided. Tons of ice fell on the ship's deck.

Below decks, water began to pour into the boiler rooms. Captain Smith took charge immediately and began an inspection of the ship. He was accompanied by the ship's designer, Thomas Andrews. It didn't take them long to realize how much damage had been done to the ship. The *Titanic* was divided into sixteen watertight compartments. Andrews explained that the ship was built to stay afloat if any of the four front compartments became flooded. If the first five compartments were flooded, however, the ship could not stay afloat. The sinking of the bow would cause water from the fifth compartment to overflow into the sixth, then the seventh, until it sank completely. At this point, five were flooded.

The passengers were unaware of what was happening below. Some had heard a crunching sound and felt a slight jarring movement, but few realized that the ship was sinking. Even when Captain Smith ordered the lifeboats to be lowered, few people believed that the ship was really in danger.

At midnight, 25 minutes after the collision, the lifeboats were lowered. But it soon became apparent that there weren't enough lifeboats for everyone on board the ship. Women and children were told to go first, but some wives decided to stay with their husbands. The first boat that was lowered could have held 65 people, but it left with only 28 passengers. At 2:00 A.M., there were still more than 1,500 people left on the sinking ship. The passengers on the stern huddled together and waved good-bye to those who were in the lifeboats.

By this time the angle of the ship had become more vertical as its propellers swung out of the water. The lights of the ship were kept on, and the band played party tunes at first. Then it played a single hymn. Suddenly the ship rose out of the water as the front tipped forward. People started falling off the deck into the freezing water. A great roar was heard as objects slid around inside the ship.

Within minutes the *Titanic* had sunk into the ocean and disappeared. Although lifeboats picked up a few people who were struggling in the cold water, most of the people who had been left on board drowned when the great ship went down at about 2:20 A.M. Of the *Titanic*'s 2,227 passengers, only 705 lived to tell the sad story. They were rescued by a ship called the *Carpathia*.

The world was shocked by the disaster, yet many people dreamed of finding the *Titanic*. Most people, however, believed that the ship had sunk far too deep to be recovered. Also, the North Atlantic was too dark, cold, and dangerous. No diver could survive a search for the wreck.

The "unsinkable" *Titanic* had gone down in the most dangerous stretch of the northwest Atlantic. For years it sat silently on the ocean's bottom, 2½ miles below the surface. Although many people dreamed of finding it, no underwater equipment could detect the wreck and no one knew where the search should begin.

Even though the exact location of the *Titanic* was still a mystery, treasure hunters had many ideas for raising the ship once it had been found. One suggested attaching a gigantic hydrogen balloon to the ship's deck and floating it to the surface. There was also a scheme to wrap a net around the *Titanic* and pump nitrogen into the net. The nitrogen would freeze and the ship would float to the surface enclosed in an enormous ice cube. Another idea was to fill the *Titanic* with Ping-Pong balls and float it to the surface!

In early 1980, a Texas millionaire spent more than $2 million on three different expeditions trying to locate the *Titanic* and salvage it. All three attempts failed, and the man ran out of money before he could locate the wreck.

The person who finally found the *Titanic* was Dr. Robert Ballard. Ballard is a scientist, an adventurer, and an underwater explorer. While he was in the U.S. Navy, he learned to dive and worked with submarines and small undersea robots. Later he took a job as a marine geologist at the Woods Hole Oceanographic Institute in Massachusetts. Ballard had always been fascinated by the story of the *Titanic*. He had no interest in salvaging treasure of any kind from the *Titanic*. In fact, he made a promise to himself that he wouldn't keep or sell anything he found on the ship. He simply wanted to visit the wreck at the bottom of the ocean.

Ballard knew that if he found the ship, it would be impossible to dive to the wreck without special equipment. The wreck was too deep to visit using only SCUBA gear. He would have to explore the *Titanic* and film the wreck from inside a submarine. His dream became a reality when the U.S. Navy agreed to sponsor the Ballard expedition. Ballard could find the *Titanic* and test special underwater equipment for the navy at the same time.

Ballard started his search where the *Titanic*'s

lifeboat passengers had been rescued the day after the ship sank. He then narrowed the position of the *Titanic* down from 130 square miles to about 30 square miles. Next he lowered a device called the *Argo* into the ocean to take pictures of objects that might be part of the *Titanic*. The Argo, a cagelike robot device with cameras and lights inside, and about the size of a small automobile, was attached to the mother ship by a cable and was slowly towed above the ocean's bottom. Another robot, called the *ANGUS* (Acoustically Navigated Geological Underwater Survey), was also used. The ANGUS was equipped with *sonar,* a device used to detect objects underwater by sound waves. The ANGUS could take color pictures of the ocean's floor.

Days and weeks went by with little success. Ballard and his crew watched picture after picture of ocean sand. Since the Atlantic was extremely turbulent during the winter months, the search could be conducted only during the summer. As the summer drew to a close, the crew became bored and frustrated. Then on September 1, 1985, they were watching the video monitor as the ANGUS swept along the ocean bottom. They had been searching within a 2- or 3-mile radius of the area where it was believed that the *Titanic* had sunk. Lifeboats had been found there, and it was also from this area that the SOS, or distress, signal had been sent.

Suddenly pictures of the *Titanic* appeared on the screen! The crew were stunned and excited by what they were seeing. No one wanted to leave the monitor and get Ballard, who was reading in his cabin below. Finally the ship's cook was phoned to go below and give Ballard the news that they had found the *Titanic*.

Ballard quickly rushed to the viewing room, where he stood watching pictures of the wrecked liner. Glancing at the time, he saw that it was 2:20 A.M. It was almost at this time that the *Titanic* had sunk. Ballard and his crew were overcome with a sense of history, so they went on deck and held a memorial service to those who had died.

Soon thousands of pictures of the wreck were taken by both the Argo and ANGUS. An important fact was revealed: The ship had broken in two as it sank below the water's surface. The two pieces were lying almost 2,000 feet apart. But Ballard and his crew had run out of time. The weather was bad, so their work would have to be postponed until later. Ballard's dream of actually landing on the *Titanic* would have to wait.

In July of 1986, Ballard and his team sailed from Woods Hole, Massachusetts, and returned to the site of the *Titanic*. This time they made several dives in a small submarine called *Alvin*. A SCUBA diver could go down only as far as 437 feet. But *Alvin* could hold three people and descend to where the *Titanic* lay—12,460 feet below the ocean's surface! Once *Alvin* left the mother ship, it took it only 2½ hours to reach the *Titanic*. During this time, Ballard would explore for 4 hours, then make another 2½-hour ascent to the surface.

Attached to *Alvin* by a cable was a very small

robot called *Jason Junior,* or *JJ.* JJ was equipped with a camera and operated by remote control. It entered the *Titanic*'s interior and took many color photographs and video pictures of the different parts of the ship. Later Ballard and his team put all the separate scenes together to show a complete picture of the *Titanic.*

JJ's pictures showed the ship's grand ballroom, the exercise rooms, even the passengers' cabins. All the wood had long been eaten away, but most of the metal remained. Ballard also found the ocean floor littered with objects from the ship. There were a doll's head, shoes, wine bottles, and wash basins. Most of these things had fallen out when the hull split in two. Ballard found a safe among the rubble. He used *Alvin*'s mechanical arm to try to open the door, but it wouldn't budge. He later saw that the safe's bottom had rusted out and there was nothing inside.

Eleven days later, Ballard completed his exploration of the *Titanic.* Perhaps the most important thing he discovered was that the iceberg didn't actually puncture a hole in the *Titanic* as had been thought. Instead, the iceberg crumpled the metal plates on the outside of the ship as it slid by. This caused the bolts that held the sheets of metal in place to pop out and water to flow inside.

All over the world, people were fascinated by the discovery of the *Titanic.* Yet there was a sadness about the ghostlike ship at the bottom of the ocean, and those who had died when it went down. On his final dive, Ballard dropped a memorial plaque on the stern of the ship, where most of the passengers had been standing before the ship went down. It was dedicated to the memory of those who lost their lives on the fateful night of April 15, 1912. Ballard hoped that no one would disturb the resting place of the *Titanic*'s passengers.

However, some French explorers decided to dive for the *Titanic*'s treasure. Officials at the French Institute for Research and Exploitation of the Sea, better known as IFREMER, carried out several salvage expeditions at the site.

The French team brought up several artifacts including a ceramic vase, a crystal bottle, some silverware, and even parts of the ship. These treasures were publicly displayed on a television show called "Titanic '87."

These objects are interesting, but the real treasure of the *Titanic* is the ship itself.

5

Treasure of Myths—
Atlantis, El Dorado, and Troy

Since the beginning of time, men have searched the world for mythical cities believed to be filled with gold. There are many stories describing mysterious, unknown places filled with unbelievable riches. These tales have led people through jungles and deserts to find the mysterious cities and the treasures they contain.

One legend was told by the ancient Greek writer Plato. He wrote that there once existed a rich and powerful island kingdom. This island continent developed such a prosperous and advanced civilization that it was known as a paradise on earth. Its name was *Atlantis.*

According to the legend, Atlantis was destroyed when a huge earthquake in the ocean caused a tidal wave. The seabed opened up and swallowed the continent. The entire island and all its people disappeared into the ocean.

Treasure hunters, explorers, and scientists have

been searching for Atlantis ever since. Is Atlantis fact or fiction? Several people who claimed to have special powers said they had talked to dead Atlantians. Among them was Edgar Cayce, a psychic who was famous about 50 years ago. (A psychic is someone who believes that he or she can read other people's thoughts, relive the past, or predict the future.) Cayce said voices from the past told him that Atlantis was somewhere in the Caribbean, near the Bahama Islands.

Very few people paid any attention to Cayce's claims. Then, during the late 1960's, several airplanes disappeared in the Caribbean. This area became known as the Bermuda Triangle. Because of these strange disappearances, many people began to investigate the region. During these investigations, researchers made an interesting discovery. Off the coast of Bimini, they found huge rocks in the water. These rocks looked as if they might be walls and roads. People searching for Atlantis thought the rocks might be a key to where Atlantis could be found.

These strange underwater walls or roads were located less than ½ mile off the western shore of Bimini. Each rock weighed between 1 and 10 tons and was under 15 feet of water. Many people who saw these stones believed they might have been part of an ancient harbor. Several set out to prove that they were once part of the lost continent of Atlantis.

In 1976, Peter Tomkins led an expedition to Bimini to determine the nature of these rocks. Were they beach rocks that had been made smooth by the ocean waves, or were they man-made? Were the roads natural formations, or had the stones been moved there by humans?

Tomkins concluded that the rock formation, which closely resembled a road or wall, was really just a product of nature. The rocks had been made smooth by the erosion of the sea. The rock walls had probably been deposited there by huge ocean swells around 2,000 years ago. This dating of the rocks made them too young to be part of the legendary civilization of Atlantis.

Yet there are those who still insist that the lost island and all its treasure lie off the coast of Bimini. These treasure hunters hope to find some evidence to support their claims. They continue to search the mysterious rocks, looking for wheel ruts in the stones or some evidence of man-made materials.

Tales of lost cities and kingdoms can be found in every part of the world. Often these stories become exaggerated or distorted with time.

The legend of El Dorado tells of an ancient civilization in the Andes Mountains where the gods demanded gifts of gold. Each year slaves would row their ruler into the middle of a lake. The ruler then threw handfuls of gold, diamonds, and emeralds into the water. According to the legend, generations of rulers performed this same ceremony until an unbelievable treasure lay on the bottom of the lake.

When the Spanish came to the New World, they desperately wanted gold. They murdered the natives or forced them into slavery while stealing as much of their gold as possible. The natives tried to resist. They hid their gold in caves and buried it in the ground. By the time the Spanish learned of the legendary lake of El Dorado, it was said that the natives had thrown millions more in gold on top of the ceremonial treasure to keep the Spaniards from taking it.

Many treasure hunters have dreamed of recovering the fabled treasure of El Dorado. During the 1550's, an explorer named Cieza de León located what is believed to be the legendary lake, Lake Guatavita. The lake is about ½ mile across and is located high in the Andes Mountains in Bogota, Colombia. The lake had originally been the crater of a volcano. It had gradually filled up with melted snow that ran down from the rim.

De León wanted to drain the lake to get the treasure, but he had little success. A second treasure hunter, Hernando Quesada, had the same idea. He used native workers passing buckets of water to one another, hand to hand, in an effort to drain the lake. After months of work, the level of the water had been lowered only a few feet. Quesada soon gave up in despair and frustration.

In 1580, a Spanish merchant, Antonio de Sepulveda, tried his hand at finding the treasures of El Dorado. He used a work force of 8,000 natives, who dug a huge notch in the rim of Lake Guatavita. Since the lake sat like a bowl of soup on top of a mountain, the merchant reasoned that letting the water out would expose the treasure at the bottom. The Indians succeeded in cutting a hole in the rim of the lake, the water poured out, and the water level slowly lowered by some 65 feet. It looked as if this attempt would succeed!

De Sepulveda was very excited. He could see the mud bottom. He found a huge emerald as large as an egg on the bottom. Believing that he would soon discover the treasure trove, he sent the emerald egg to the king of Spain. Then he waited for a reward, but none came. The king would not pay a cent of reward until the lake was completely dry and the gold recovered.

Soon afterward, disaster struck. The trench collapsed and many natives were drowned as the water poured back into the lake. Broke and frustrated, de Sepulveda ended his treasure hunt and the lake was almost forgotten. But a legend that speaks of an estimated $5 billion in gold is not forgotten for long. In 1801, a French adventurer and a British sea captain joined forces to uncover the treasure. They built a canal in the side of the lake, but it collapsed from the weight of the water the very first time it was opened. Exhausted, they, too, gave up the search.

However, the greed for gold soon attracted another group of businessmen. In 1899, a young and brilliant Spanish engineer named Hernando da Villa tried his luck. He dug a huge underground tunnel right into the lake bed. After 13 years of persistent effort, he succeeded in draining the lake—a feat no one else had accomplished despite 300 years of trying.

Unfortunately, da Villa did not find the lake bottom strewn with treasure. To his dismay, what he found was 25 feet of soft, sticky, gooey mud. Workers floundered around in the gluelike substance. Even worse, once the water had been removed, the tropical sun turned the mud to concrete. If there was any treasure, it had been baked right into the cement and would now be impossible to reach. The treasure was now sealed in a layer of sun-dried brick. Before workers could drill through the hardened mud, the lake gradually began to fill up again. At that point da Villa, too, gave up. He abandoned the project when he was overcome by the same disappointment, despair, and frustration that so many others before him had felt.

Throughout the years, several other attempts were made to reach the treasures of El Dorado. During the 1930's, SCUBA divers searched the lake, but the thick mud on the bottom revealed no treasure. During the 1950's, a fortune hunter tried dragging a steel ball with claws along the lake bottom. Once again the attempt was a disaster. Other treasure hunters have tried and also failed. To this day no one has been able to find the legendary gold of El Dorado.

Stories of long-lost empires and missing treasures fill history books and inspire treasure hunters. But most of these legends are either myths or the results of stories that have grown fantastic through the years. Only the most determined adventurers have pursued these stories. Heinrich Schliemann was such an adventurer. His determination helped him to find not only a lost city but also a fabulous treasure. A dream of many years had finally come true. The city of Schliemann's dreams was Troy.

According to the ancient Greek poet Homer, a war was fought between the Greeks and the Trojans. The war lasted 10 long years without either side winning. After 10 years, the Greeks built a huge hollow horse with a secret entrance. When it was completed, some of the Greeks climbed inside and closed the entrance. The rest of the Greek warriors pretended to depart and left the horse outside the walls of Troy. The Trojans found the horse and dragged it inside their city, tearing down the protective walls surrounding the city to do so. That evening, while the Trojans slept, the Greeks climbed out of the horse and attacked them. They killed them all and burned the city of Troy to the ground.

As a boy in Germany, Schliemann had read this story over and over again. He intended to find the city of Troy and walk on the very ground where these heroes had fought. By the age of 40, Schliemann had become a millionaire several times. He decided to spend his fortune searching for the city of Troy. The few people who believed there was an actual Troy thought it might be located inside a mound somewhere in the northwest corner of Turkey. These mounds were common in the Middle East and were the result of cities being built on top of one another over hundreds of years.

In 1870, Schliemann traveled to Turkey and began his search. During his journey, he read and reread Homer's story for clues to Troy's location. According to the story, the Greeks had traveled back and forth to their ships, so Troy must have been located near the sea. Homer's story also mentioned a terrible fight between heroes on each side. In the fight, a Greek hero chased a Trojan hero around the outer walls of the city three times.

Schliemann found an area that seemed to fit the description of Troy's landscape almost exactly. He then hired hundreds of workers and began to dig a big trench through the middle of the mound. After digging only a few feet, the workers began to find pieces of pottery. After 3 years, they reached the bottom of the mound. Schliemann counted as many as *nine* cities that had been built on top of one another. But he found no treasure.

According to Homer, the king of Troy had had a wonderful treasure of gold. Yet after a great deal of searching, Schliemann found no evidence of it. On the very day that he was about to leave, however, Schliemann spotted a glistening object sticking out from between two stones. Gold jewelry! When Schliemann pulled the object from the wall, he realized that he had found his treasure!

Schliemann immediately gave all the workmen the day off and waited until he and his wife, Sophie, were alone. They then dug into the stone wall with knives and shovels, pulling out more and more golden objects. They eventually found more than 8,000 gold items—including necklaces, bracelets, cups, and vases. They stopped digging only when the wall itself was about to collapse on them.

Schliemann believed he had found the city of Troy and its treasure, but he had not. He had dug right through the city of Troy, as was later discovered, to an even *earlier* city!

Schliemann placed the golden objects he had found on display and even dressed his wife in the golden jewelry for photographers. Then he secretly took the gold out of Turkey and gave it to a German museum. When World War II started, the Germans hid the treasure beneath some gardens in Berlin. When the war ended, the gold could not be found. It had disappeared completely. Some say the Nazis melted down the ancient objects and used the gold to finance their war. Others say that the Russians, who were the first to enter the city after the war, dug up the gold and took it to Moscow. But no one knows for sure. All we know is that the treasure vanished and has never been found.

6

Treasures of War

During times of war, wealthy people sometimes hid their valuables underground or in caves for safekeeping. Armies frequently stole the enemy's treasures to help pay for the cost of the war. Some of these hidden valuables have now been found, but many have been lost or forgotten.

In the late 1930's, Germany was ruled by the Nazis. World War II started in 1939, when Germany invaded Poland. Soon Germany had also invaded France, the Netherlands, and most of Europe. Immediately following these invasions, German agents looted the cathedrals, museums, and homes of the wealthy. They took priceless artwork, jewels, and gold and shipped them back to Germany, where they vanished into secret hiding places.

As the war turned against them, the Nazi leaders began to hoard the stolen valuables for themselves. They hoped to reclaim these riches after the war was over. Experts estimate that the Nazis may have stolen more than $500 billion in gold *alone.*

In 1945, a victorious U.S. Army unit was going through a small town in Austria when an elderly man ran toward them. The old man was extremely excited and pulled at the American lieutenant. An American soldier who could spcak Gcrman camc forward to translate. The old man then told them of a nearby salt mine, Merkers Mine, that was filled with treasure.

The lieutenant followed the old man into a building and down a long corridor. At the end of the corridor was the entrance to the salt mine. Its walls shimmered with salt crystals. The German picked up a lantern, lit it, then led the Americans down a long passageway. Cautious at first, the American lieutenant drew his revolver and followed. The old man opened a door leading to a room along the side of the tunnel. He shined his light inside.

The lieutenant squinted his eyes and peered into the darkness. He couldn't believe what he saw. Before him were masses of gold and silver objects, valuable paintings against each wall, and beautiful marble statues! And this was just the beginning. The Americans opened room after room to find more treasure than they had ever imagined. What they were looking at were the treasures that had been looted by the Nazis. The treasures had been hidden away in Merkers Mine to keep them from being destroyed while U.S. forces bombed Germany.

The mine turned out to be a good place in which to store the artwork. The temperature never went above 47 degrees, summer or winter. The oil paintings had survived the war and were well preserved.

Soon after the mine was discovered, art experts from all over the world came to Austria to catalog the pieces, as well as to determine their original owners. All of the experts were astonished at what they saw—objects of art that had been stolen from private collectors and museums all over Europe. In one chamber they found the crown jewels of the Holy Roman Empire, a treasure that dated to the Middle Ages. In the same chamber there was a priceless statue created by Michelangelo, along with his painting of the Madonna and Child.

The other rooms contained paintings by many famous artists, including Michelangelo and Raphael. In all, 6,000 very valuable paintings were recovered! Yet the strangest discovery was nearly missed. It was hidden at the back of Merkers Mine. A small chamber had been made to look like a shrine. Inside were the coffins of Germany's past leaders—including those of Frederick the Great and his father, Frederick William, both of whom were German emperors. The coffins of World War I hero Field Marshal Paul von Hindenburg and his wife had been placed along the walls. Banners from famous German regiments hung from the ceiling and decorated the walls.

All the rooms in the entire cave were littered with boxes of dynamite. All the boxes were hooked together so that one button would trigger the explosives. Hitler had intended to destroy everything rather than turn them over to his enemies!

The discoveries of Merkers Mine were only the

beginning. All over Germany and Austria, experts began to find treasure that had been stolen and hidden by the Nazis. At Neuschwanstein Castle in Bavaria, the Allies found hundreds of gold objects. They then went to a copper mine in Westphalia, where an elevator took them 2,000 feet underground. There they found piles of valuable antiques, elaborate furniture, and lamps.

At Nuremberg, the Allies found the diamond-and-ruby-studded crown of Charlemagne hidden in an air-raid shelter. Charlemagne, or Charles the Great, was crowned the first emperor of France and Germany in A.D. 800. Along with his crown, they found his shield, two of his swords, and his scepter.

In April 1945, during the last days of Hitler's rule, there was a rumor that a plane carrying gold, platinum, and official documents had left Berlin for Hitler's hideout in Austria. The plane never arrived. It was believed to have been shot down by Allied fighter planes. If this is really what happened, the plane probably crashed either in the Austrian mountains near Lake Toplitz or in the lake itself.

Although the Austrian government immediately began a search for the plane, they found nothing. Years later, during the 1950's, several strange events took place in the area of Lake Toplitz. In one case, two climbers were found stabbed to death near a series of holes that had been dug in the ground. The holes appeared to be attempts to dig up treasure.

In 1960, a German magazine sponsored a salvage operation in Lake Toplitz to locate the Nazi treasure. But instead of finding gold, the magazine's search brought up a sealed trunk filled with fake British money. The Austrian government immediately took over the search effort. In 1963, they found twelve more chests filled with counterfeit British pound notes and two chests containing thirty-two counterfeit plates. They also brought up a case of printing equipment.

The curious Austrians then searched through wartime Nazi records. What they found was amazing. During the last years of the war the Germans began a project that they had code-named Operation Burnhard. The plan was to destroy the British money system by flooding England with fake money. The money was to be printed in German concentration-camp factories and then smuggled into England. With so much fake money around, the real money would become worthless. Nobody would have known whether the English money they had was real or fake, so none of it could be trusted. Businesses wouldn't want to accept English money because it could prove to be worthless.

Apparently the operation was never carried out. But what were the plates doing in the middle of the Austrian lake? And what happened to the valuables that were supposed to have been on Hitler's plane? Many people think that the officers in charge of the fake money scheme had intended to use the counterfeit money themselves after the war. But the fate of the mysterious treasure plane, if it ever actually existed, has never been discovered. Some say that the Nazi treasure may still be out there, just waiting to be found.

Afterword

In this book you have read stories of mysterious treasure hunts and stories of people who spent their lives pursuing one special goal—the discovery of hidden treasure. But by now you may also realize that treasure can be found anywhere and anytime. There might be treasure buried in your own attic or cellar. It could be a collection of old stamps, or the rare signature of a famous person on an old letter or book.

Sometimes people even stumble over treasure without realizing it. For example, on the West Coast of the United States, you might find a beautiful iridescent glass ball on the beach. These beautiful glass balls are used by some local Japanese fishermen as floats on their nets. They are collector's items and are worth a great deal of money.

Even old schoolbooks can become collector's items. An author who is unknown today may become world-famous within 20 years. Seashells that are unusual or oddly shaped can be collected. You might even be lucky enough to find a *fossil* (the hardened imprint, or traces, of animals or plants) in a field near your home. So look around. Something may be waiting for you to discover it. Then you, too, will understand the thrill of the hunt for treasure!

Other titles in the Explorer Books series